YOUR BODY inside and out

Senses

Angela Royston

W
FRANKLIN WATTS
LONDON · SYDNEY

Franklin Watts
Published in Great Britain in 2015 by
The Watts Publishing Group

Series editor: Sarah Peutrill
Art director: Jonathan Hair
Design: Mo Choy
Illustrator: Ian Thompson
Consultant: Peter Riley
Photographs: Paul Bricknell, unless otherwise credited

Picture credits: Andy Crawford: 7, 8t,10,22. Joe
Bator/Corbis: 13cl. John Birdsall Photo Library: 13r, 19.
Paul Doyle/Photofusion: 29. Keystone/Topfoto: 18.

Every attempt has been made to clear copyright.
Should there be any inadvertent omission please apply
to the publisher for rectification.

A CIP catalogue record for this book is available from
the British Library.

Dewey number: 612.8
ISBN: 978 1 4451 3887 9

Printed in China

Franklin Watts
An imprint of
Hachette Children's Group
Part of The Watts Publishing Group
Carmelite House
50 Victoria Embankment
London EC4Y 0DZ

An Hachette UK Company
www.hachette.co.uk

www.franklinwatts.co.uk

MIX
Paper from
responsible sources
FSC® C104740

Contents

What are the senses?

Your senses tell you about the world around you. Your senses involve parts of your body you can see, and parts that are hidden inside you.

Getting information

You use all your senses when you eat an apple. You feel the apple in your hand, and you see and smell it before you take a bite.

◀ As you take a bite, you taste the fruit and hear the sound of the apple crunching between your teeth.

Ear------------•

Tongue

Sense organs

You collect information about the world using your eyes, ears, nose, tongue and skin. These parts of your body are called your sense organs.

You see with your eyes, ▶
hear with your ears,
smell with your nose,
taste with your tongue
and feel with your skin.

Brain-----------

Eye--------

Nose-----------

Skin----------

Your brain

Your sense organs collect information about the world and send it along nerves inside your body to your brain. Your brain makes sense of all the information it receives.

Nerve endings

Nerve endings in your sense organs collect a particular kind of information. Nerve endings in your eyes, for example, react to light, not to sound.

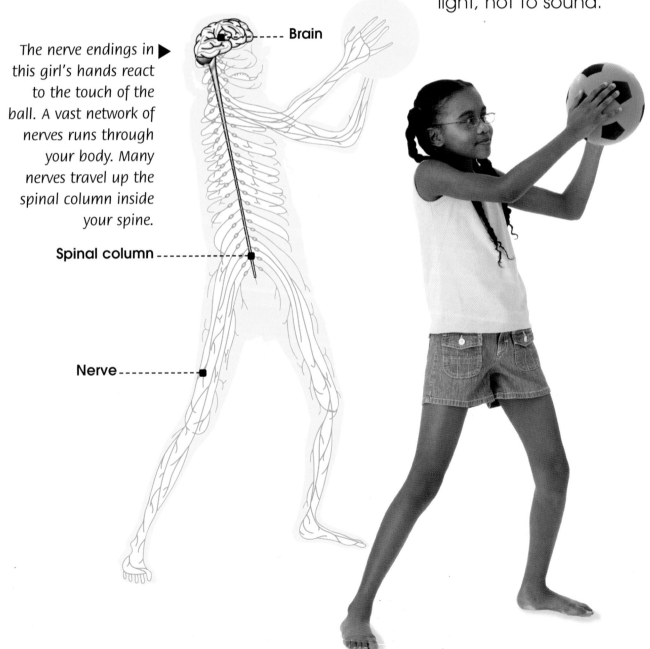

The nerve endings in ▶ this girl's hands react to the touch of the ball. A vast network of nerves runs through your body. Many nerves travel up the spinal column inside your spine.

---- **Brain**

Spinal column -------------

Nerve -------------

The brain

The brain controls your whole body. It receives information from your sense organs and it tells the rest of your body what to do.

Different parts of the brain control ▶ different things, such as seeing, hearing and thinking.

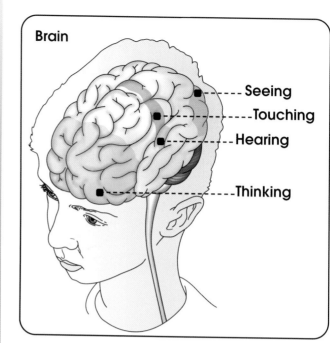

Brain

Seeing
Touching
Hearing

Thinking

Supercomputer

Your brain is a bit like a computer – it takes in and uses information. But a computer can't do many of the things your brain does, such as feel happy or lonely.

◀ *Playing a computer game involves seeing, hearing and touching. Signals from your eyes, ears and hands go to different places in your brain.*

Seeing

You see only when light enters your eyes. If you shut your eyes, you block out the light and cannot see anything. Your eyes control how much light goes into them.

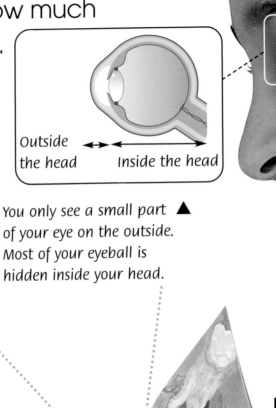

Outside the head ↔ Inside the head

You only see a small part ▲ of your eye on the outside. Most of your eyeball is hidden inside your head.

How light reaches your eyes

You have to look at something in the light to see it. Light bounces off the things you are looking at and goes into your eyes.

The pupil

Light goes into your eye through the pupil. This is the round black hole in the middle of the coloured iris. The iris controls how much light goes inside your eye.

The iris is made of ▶ *muscles. The iris makes the pupil smaller in bright light. In dim light (picture below), the iris makes the pupil larger to let in more light.*

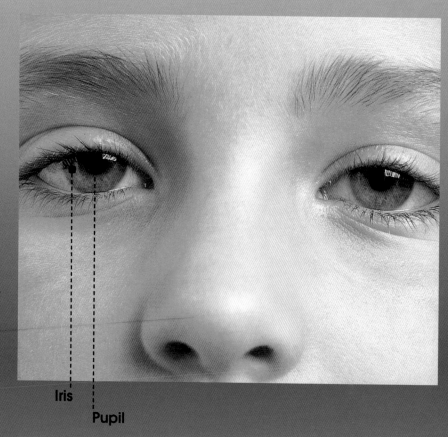

Iris

Pupil

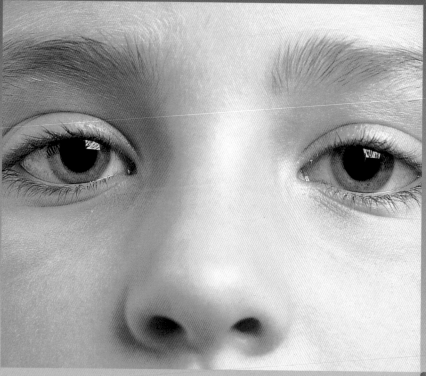

Try this!

Look at your eyes in a mirror. Are the pupils large or small? Look at them again in dim light. Have they changed?

Inside the eye

Light goes through your eye and forms a picture on the retina on the back of your eyeball. The picture on the retina is upside down. The retina changes the light into electrical signals that go along a nerve to your brain. When your brain receives the information it turns the picture the right way up.

Making a clear picture
The inside of your eye works like a camera. The lens bends the light so that it forms a clear picture on the retina.

The lens is just behind the iris. The retina stretches around the inside of the back of your eye. Most of the space inside your eye is filled with a kind of jelly.
▼

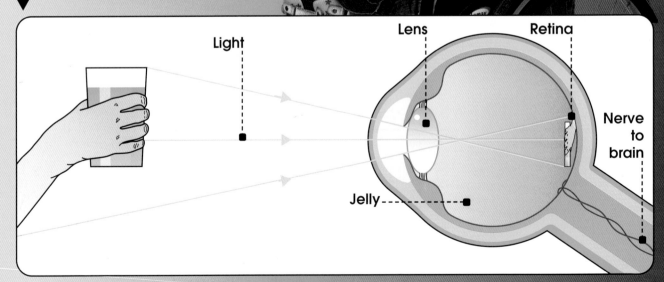

Light

Lens

Retina

Nerve to brain

Jelly

Seeing colour

The retina has millions of nerve endings. Only some nerve endings see different colours. The other nerve endings see shapes in black and grey.

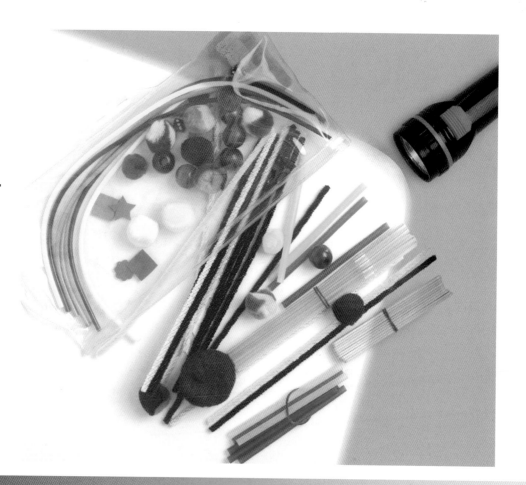

The nerve endings ▶ in the retina that see colour work best in bright light. That is why things look grey or black at night.

Colour blind

Some people cannot tell the difference between some colours. For example, the colours red and green may look the same to a person who is colour blind.

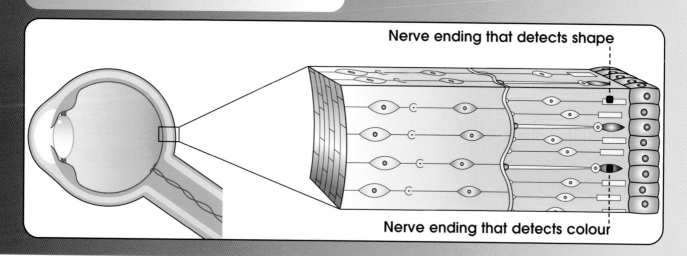

Nerve ending that detects shape

Nerve ending that detects colour

Wearing glasses

Some people's eyes do not make a clear picture on their retinas. These people wear glasses or contact lenses to help them see clearly.

How glasses work

Short-sighted people can see things well that are near to them, but they cannot see things clearly that are far away. Glasses bend the light so that the person can see more clearly.

Image on retina

Lens of eye   Lens of glasses   Tin

Blindness

People who are blind can see very little, or even nothing at all. This may be because the retina, or the nerve to the brain, is damaged.

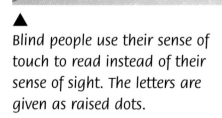

▲
Blind people use their sense of touch to read instead of their sense of sight. The letters are given as raised dots.

Sunglasses

Sunlight can harm your eyes. Everyone should wear sunglasses in strong sunlight to protect their eyes.

▲
Some blind people have a specially trained dog to guide them when they go outside. Others carry a white stick to feel the ground ahead of them.

Hearing

You hear through your ears. You can hear sounds from all around you, even behind your head. Sounds can travel through air, water and solid things, like walls and doors.

Making a noise

When something makes a noise, it sends sound waves through the air. Sound waves carry the noise to your ears. When a sound wave hits something it makes it shake, or vibrate.

The eardrum

When sound waves reach your ears, your ear flaps direct them into your ear canal. This tube leads to your eardrum. The sound waves make your eardrum vibrate.

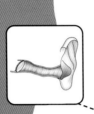

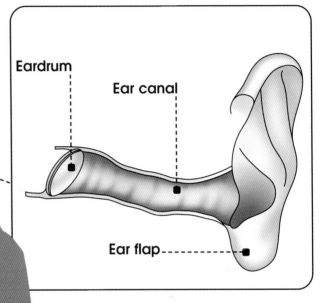

Eardrum

Ear canal

Ear flap

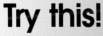

▲
Your ears are on the side of your head, but the parts that you see are only flaps of skin and gristle. Your ears go deep inside your head.

▲
The eardrum is a sheet of skin that stretches across your ear canal. The eardrum is quite thin so do not poke things down your ear canal.

Try this!

Bang a drum with a drum stick. Put your other hand on the flat part of the drum. Can you feel it vibrating?

Inside your ear

Sound vibrations pass from the eardrum through the middle ear to the inner ear. Part of the inner ear contains nerves that tell your brain about sounds. The other part helps you to balance.

Journey through the ear
The eardrum is attached to a chain of small bones. Vibrations pass through the bones to the inner ear. The louder the sound is, the stronger the vibrations.

When liquid in the inner ear vibrates, nerve endings send signals to the brain.
▼

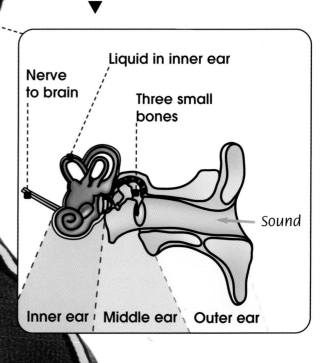

Nerve
to brain

Liquid in inner ear

Three small
bones

Sound

Inner ear | Middle ear | Outer ear

Balancing

Your inner ears help you to balance. The semicircular canals are three tubes filled with liquid. The sides of the tubes are lined with nerve endings.

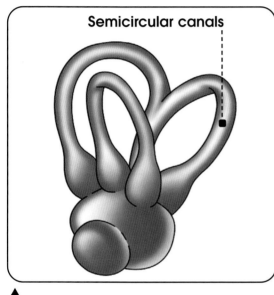

Semicircular canals

▲

Whenever you move, the liquid inside the semicircular canals moves too. The nerves pass signals to your brain so that you know which way your body is tilted.

Try this!

Spin around on the spot on a soft surface such as grass. Then stop suddenly. Do you feel dizzy? This is because the liquid in the semicircular canals is still spinning.

Hard of hearing

Some people's ears do not work well and so they find it hard to hear. People who are hard of hearing can hear loud sounds, but deaf people cannot hear what people are saying.

Hard of hearing

People who are hard of hearing use a hearing aid to help them hear better. The hearing aid makes the sounds louder and clearer.

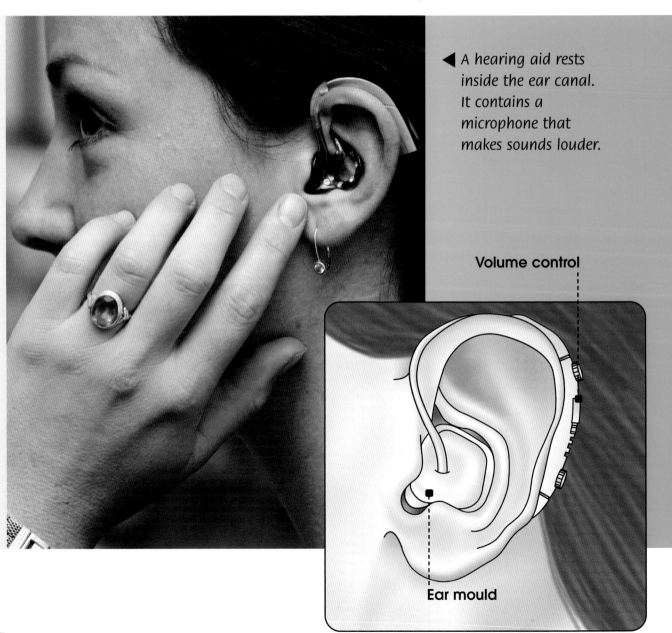

◀ A hearing aid rests inside the ear canal. It contains a microphone that makes sounds louder.

Volume control

Ear mould

Deafness

Some people are too deaf for a hearing aid to help them. They may watch people's lips to tell what they are saying, or they may speak using sign language.

▲
You can learn sign language whether you are deaf or not. Some hand signs spell out words, others have separate signs for whole words.

Smelling

You smell as your breathe in air through your nose. As the air goes through your nose to your lungs, nerve endings in your nose detect any smells.

Making a smell
Something smells when it gives off gas or tiny particles that float in the air. Some things, such as flowers and perfume, smell nice, but some other things smell nasty.

When you bite an ▶ orange, a fine spray of juice floats into the air. Some of the spray goes inside your nose with the air you breathe in.

Detecting smell

The nerve endings that pick up smells are inside the highest part of your nose. Sniffing helps you smell better, because sniffing pulls more air to the top of your nose.

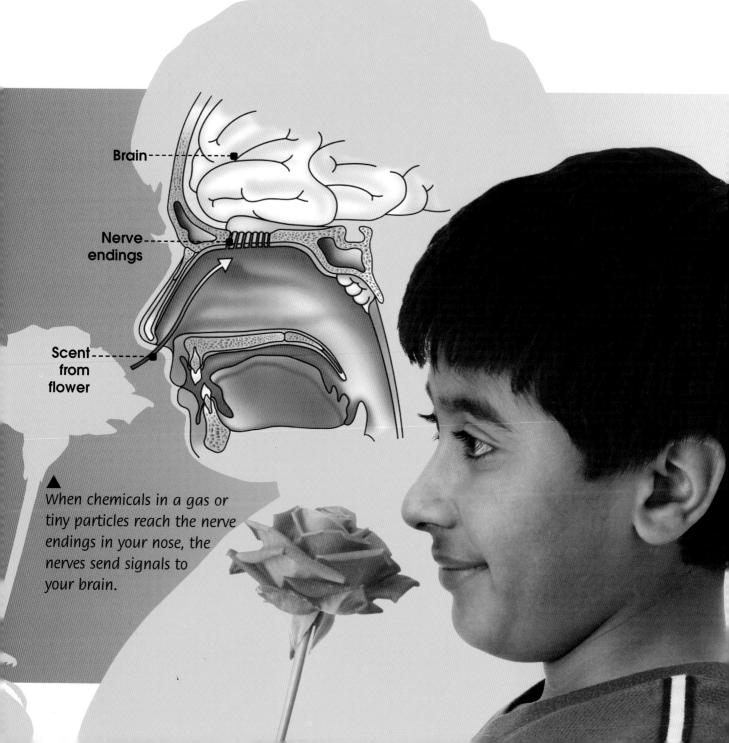

Brain

Nerve endings

Scent from flower

▲ When chemicals in a gas or tiny particles reach the nerve endings in your nose, the nerves send signals to your brain.

Tasting

You taste when you lick something, sip a liquid, or chew up food. Most of the nerve endings that tell you about taste are buried in your tongue.

Taste buds

Your tongue and the inside of your mouth are coated with saliva. Tiny bits of food and drink mix with the saliva and trickle into your taste buds.

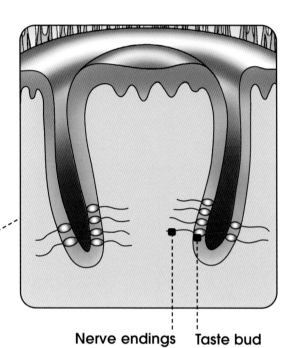

Nerve endings   Taste bud

▲
Your tongue is covered with tiny bumps. The bumps contain taste buds with nerve endings. The nerve endings send signals to your brain about the things you taste.

Try this!

Hold your nose and eat a piece of cheese. Now let go of your nose and have another bite. Does the smell help you taste it better?

Combining tastes

We think that different things taste very different, but every taste is mainly salty, sweet, sour or bitter, or a mixture of them. Most people like sweet or salty things best.

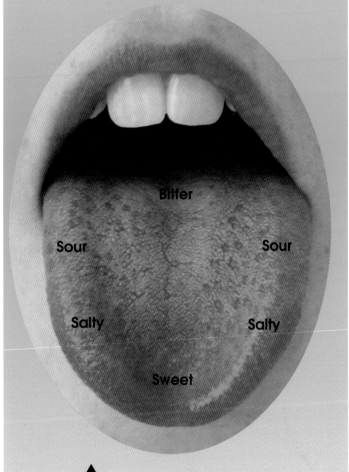

Bitter

Sour   Sour

Salty   Salty

Sweet

▲
The taste buds on some parts of your tongue detect mainly one kind of taste more than others.

Heat and pain

The nerve endings near the surface of your skin tell you whether things are hot or cold. Other nerve endings also tell you about heat and yet others make you feel pain.

Hot and cold

The parts of your body that are sensitive to touch are also sensitive to temperature. Some parts of your skin are particularly sensitive to heat.

Nerve endings for heat

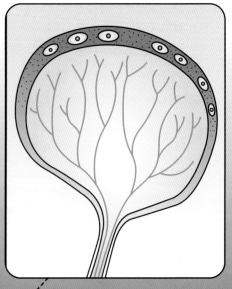

◀ If you test warm water with your hand and your elbow, it will feel warmer to your elbow. This is because your elbow has more nerve endings that are sensitive to heat.

In pain

Special nerve endings sense pain. You have nerve endings for pain in your stomach, muscles and many places inside your body. They tell you when something is wrong.

Nerve endings for pain

When you bump your knee, it ▶ hurts. Nerve endings for pain send messages to your brain.

Try this!

Before you next jump into the swimming pool, test the water with your hand and then with your foot. Does it feel colder to one of them?

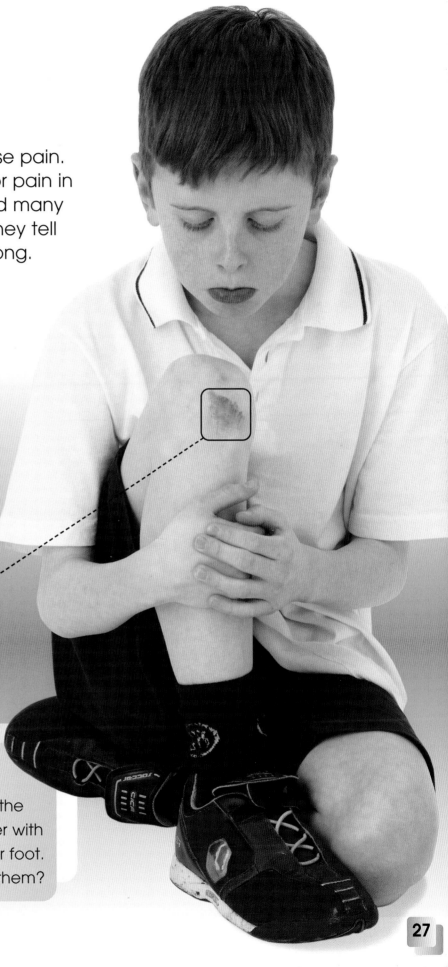

Working together

Your senses work together. If you hear a noise you look to see what made it. Sight, hearing and touch are the senses you use the most.

Using your senses

All the time you are awake your brain is receiving information through your senses. Your brain decides which messages are important, and what you should do.

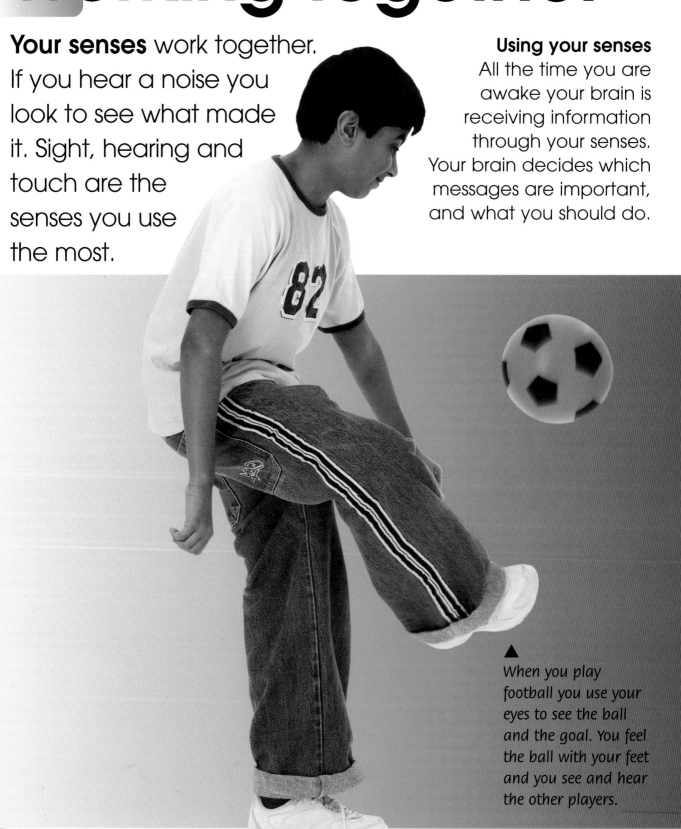

▲ When you play football you use your eyes to see the ball and the goal. You feel the ball with your feet and you see and hear the other players.

Managing without a sense

If you lose one of your senses, the other senses often become better. Blind people use hearing and touch instead of sight, while deaf people rely on their sense of sight.

Touching is comforting

Your senses can affect how you feel. Hugging someone can make you feel happy. Stroking a pet can make you feel calm.

Blind people rely on their sense of smell and touch. This blind gardener can identify plants with touch and smell.

▼

Glossary

Brain
The part of the body that receives information from your senses and controls most of your body.

Contact lens
A curved piece of plastic that acts as a lens and floats on top of the eye to help people see better.

Ear canal
The tube that leads from the flap of skin on the side of the head to the eardrum.

Eardrum
A thin layer of skin that stretches across the bottom of the ear canal.

Electrical signals
Short blips of electricity.

Gas
Small, invisible particles that float in the air.

Hearing aid
A device that fits in the ear and helps people to hear better.

Inner ear
The part of your ear that is deepest inside your head. It contains nerve endings that send signals to your brain about sounds.

Lens
A curved object that makes light bend.

Short-sighted
When things that are near to your eyes are clear but things that are further away look blurred.

Microphone
A device that makes sounds louder.

Middle ear
Three small bones that vibrate to pass sounds from the eardrum to the inner ear.

Nerve
A thin fibre that passes electrical signals from the sense organs to the brain. (A different kind of nerve passes signals from the brain to the muscles.)

Nerve endings
The ends of a nerve that collect electrical signals to send to the brain.

Particles
Very small bits of something, which are usually too small to see.

Pupil
The black hole in the centre of your eye that lets in light.

Retina
The area at the back of the eyeball which is filled with nerve endings.

Semicircular canals
Three tubes in the inner ear that help you to balance.

Sense organ
A particular part of the body that collects information about the world.

Sensitive
Easily affected.

Sign language
A way of talking using your hands.

Sound waves
Vibrations that your ears hear as sounds.

Spinal column
A bundle of nerves that goes up the middle of your spine.

Spine
The series of bones that run vertically up your back.

Taste buds
A collection of nerve endings, mainly in your tongue.

Vibrate
To shake or quiver very fast.

FURTHER INFORMATION: WEBSITES

www.childrensuniversity.manchester. ac.uk/interactives/science/brainand senses gives you information and activities about the senses

www.kidshealth.org gives you information about your body. Click on the section called 'for kids'

Index